A Woman's Voice

~ Inspirational Short Stories ~

Volume 1

DOLORES AYOTTE

A Woman's Voice (Inspirational Short Stories) Volume 1

Copyright © 2012 by Dolores Ayotte. All rights reserved.

No part of this publication may be reproduced, stored in a retrieval system or transmitted in any way by any means, electronic, mechanical, photocopy, recording or otherwise without the prior permission of the author except as provided by Canada and United States copyright law.

Book design copyright © 2012 by Dolores Ayotte. All rights reserved.

Cover design by Dolores Ayotte

Cover photo by Shirley Gauthier Sarafinchan

Interior design by Dolores Ayotte

Printed by CreateSpace

Published in Canada

ISBN: 978-0-9948673-1-5

Self-Help, Motivational & Inspirational

Disclaimer: The suggestions provided in this inspirational book are based on a personal point of view and not in any professional capacity.

Dolores Ayotte ~ The Human & Humane Self-Help Author

Dolores holds a Bachelor of Arts degree with a major in psychology from the University of Winnipeg as well as teacher certification from the University of Manitoba. She has also taken courses in human relationships and communication.

Her self-help books are written in retrospect based on a proven recipe, one she has incorporated step by step into her own life. Over time, Dolores eventually developed better life coping skills which inspired her to put pen to paper and write three previous books about her experiences. She utilizes quotes, anecdotes, humor and her own personal stories when necessary to make her suggestions relevant and to give an example of how to use her simple tips in daily living.

She is now retired and spends half the year with her husband at a retirement community in Arizona. For the remainder of the year, Dolores enjoys her children and grandchildren in Winnipeg, Manitoba where she was born and raised. She continues to learn from all the people who touch her life.

Table of Contents

Introduction

1. The Empty Nest
2. Unconditional Love versus Conditional Love
3. The Big Copout
4. You Are Not Broken ~ Andrea Ayotte Cockerill
5. He's Got the Whole World in His Hands
6. The Jongleur
7. The Three R's
8. Confidence in God
9. First Things First
10. Psst…Hey Ewe!
11. The Absence Of
12. Love Triangle ~ Fred Ayotte
13. Positive Attitude
14. The Truth
15. On Being Judgmental
16. Connecting the Dots
17. Child's Play…or is it?
18. Found Money
19. Drip…Drop ~ A Christmas Thought
20. Christmas Love

Conclusion

Sample Chapter – A Woman's Voice ~ Volume 2 ~
    Chapter 17 ~ Having a Bad Day
Sample Chapter – A Woman's Voice ~ Volume 3 ~
    Chapter 25 ~ Common Courtesy
Sample Chapter - Growing Up and Liking It ~ Chapter 3
    ~ **My *No* Means *No*!**

Introduction

As I enter into my twilight years, I want to permanently shed my insecurities and enter this final stage of my life with as much grace and wisdom as humanly possible. I have been an observant student for the majority of my life. Perhaps now, after all these years, I can get into the driver's seat and call myself a good teacher. I have succeeded in learning to "teach without classroom walls" and I have now written my own motivational books to go along with this philosophy. This experience has been extremely liberating for me. I hope by reading what I have to say and by incorporating some of my suggestions into your life, you too can find a sense of true freedom and peace.

At the end of each chapter, there is an opportunity for personal reflection. I recommend that you take a moment to personally consider the questions posed and how my words can make a difference in your life. As you can see by this lovely cover, a photo generously provided by my talented sister Shirley Gauthier Sarafinchan, the reflection in the water can be seen as a gentle reminder that as life goes on we have many opportunities to live, learn, and reflect on life in general. We also have every opportunity to learn from these reflections to help ensure that history doesn't repeat itself.

There is no need to rush through this inspirational book. It is meant to be read slowly, pondered upon, used as a stepping stone to reflect upon its content, its message and how it applies to each of you in your own life. I also want you to realize that my voice is only a soft whisper. Please hear it this way. It's from my heart to yours. Maya Angelou's words mirror my exact sentiments. *"The idea is to write it so that people hear it and it slides through the brain and goes straight to the heart".*

"When the wish for peace is genuine, the means for finding it is given in a form each mind that seeks for it in honesty can understand." ~ Helen Schucman & William Thetford

1 ~ The Empty Nest

The house is quiet as we both go about our usual business. We are never alone despite the silence that endures between us. This is a result of a true and unending love relationship that started as a friendship between my husband and me.

After over forty years of marriage, sharing a home, first only with each other…then raising a family, we sit in the peaceful silence of our empty nest knowing that this is our quiet time together. We have not entered our twilight years lightly nor without great thought and careful planning. We know that we are on the home stretch of, not only our years together, but of our very lives. We have more years to look back on than ahead. It is good…in fact, it is more than good, it is all that I could have ever dreamed of or hoped for in the life that has been given to me. I am forever grateful to have been given so much. I take nothing for granted and each day I thank God for my many blessings.

Some refer to this stage of life as the "empty nest" while I prefer to see it as the stage of life when we can sit back and be grateful for having survived its challenges. It is not an easy feat to simultaneously marry young, educate ourselves, and raise a family. We all go through the growing pains that must take place in order to accomplish and succeed in our efforts to have a successful marriage. Yet, I'm not so sure what appears to be a successful marriage is always a happy one…by that, I mean would you do it all over again if the choice was yours to make?

At this moment in time, I find myself more content and reflective. I not only have embraced this quiet time of my life, I have worked towards it. This opportunity leads to numerous seeds ready to germinate into the little stories I so deeply enjoy sharing. Not too long ago, one of my fellow authors suggested it would be a great book idea to write about the ingredients that make up a really good marriage, not a marriage that one endures but rather a holy union that one would eagerly say "yes" to again if they had to start all over.

Take a moment to just sit there and reflect. Think about the person you are married to and how you view him/her. Just between you and your Maker, would you honestly marry this person again? Be really honest now? Remember, if you can't be honest in this personal quiet time when you look at your spouse, it will be very difficult for you to be honest in your relationship. So…would you actually marry your spouse knowing all that you do today? I'm just asking for a simple 'yes or no'. No more, no less. I don't want to hear a maybe because it implies that you want your spouse to change. That's not what this is all about. Plain and simple…would you marry your spouse again if given a second chance to choose otherwise?

If the answer is a resounding no, then my next question is why? Is your spouse such a disappointment to you that if given a second chance you might say 'no' or 'maybe if'? Is it really about misplaced expectations or is it about not knowing what true love really is? A relative once stated that I had a perfect marriage. I would have to disagree. To have a perfect marriage implies perfection or a union of two perfect people. Most of us know full well that such a concept is absolutely impossible and does not exist, at least not on this side of the turf…but I do believe in perfect love. To me, perfect love is learning to love and accept your spouse no matter what. All you need to do is refer to those old-fashioned marriage vows to get my drift. Do you still believe in those words…if so, you are on the right track? All you need to do is visualize yourself riding off into the sunset with your better half. If you can do this…the sky's the limit.

"Love means the body, the soul, the life, the entire being. We feel love as we feel the warmth of our blood, we breathe love as we breathe the air, we hold it in ourselves as

we hold our thoughts. Nothing more exists for us." ~ Guy De Maupassant

"How you react towards your spouse is a choice rooted in your heart." ~ Jim Hughes

2 ~ Unconditional Love versus Conditional Love

A friend of mine has been having a difficult time the last couple of months. She has a married son. He is her only child and he also has one son, her only grandchild. They live several hundred miles apart; therefore, she doesn't see this precious little family very often. As a result, my friend has gotten to know her infant grandchild very well through the use of Skype and other means of communication with her son and daughter-in-law. However, the last time they came home to visit, there was an unfortunate turn of events and things did not go well. Now, the communication is no longer the same. There is no more Skyping and the emails are few and far between. She mentioned something that prompted me to write this article. She said that when they do communicate, that the "sign off" is now different. They don't always "sign off" with their name or they don't "sign off" with the word "love" anymore. I find this very odd.

I have also had the misfortune of unsmooth relationships in my life. How about you? Please bear with me as I ask a few more questions. Does anyone really know and understand the meaning of "**un**conditional love"? In actuality, "**un**conditional love" is just that…no conditions, whether tacit or verbal, when offering our love to others. It is what I refer to as "perfect love" or acceptance. We all know that there is no such thing as perfect people. If the love we have for others is based on the expectation of perfection or requires others to conform to our way of thinking, it is doomed to fail.

So I dare to ask, what kind of love do you offer? Loved based on conditions is really not love at all. In my opinion, it is kind of like a pseudo-love whereby it must be earned in order to receive it or we must behave in a certain manner in order to be worthy of it. When someone upsets us and we still need to communicate for whatever reason, it may be merely as simple as looking at how we now "sign off" in our communication with them after the altercation. Take a moment to think about it and you will know exactly what I mean. We really can be a lot more apparent than we realize.

It can be likened to child's play…I won't love you anymore if…I won't play with you anymore if…I won't help you anymore if…

Have you altered your relationships and now wonder why things are different? Try to keep in mind that for every action…there is a reaction. Have you changed your "sign off" with some members of your family or friends? How have other things changed and why? Have you spoken "about" the person instead of "to" the person? Simple questions but…they are not so easy to answer. It is very difficult to take responsibility for our part in unsmooth relationships.

It's easy to love someone when we agree. To love "**un**conditionally" is to love others like God loves us. The true test comes when we don't agree and there are no ifs, ands, or buts about it. This is "**un**conditional love" and it makes a whole world of difference in how we treat others.

"To love is a beautiful, mysterious event; do not miss it. Be neither too cautious nor too absorbed. Too many of us reason with our hearts and experience with our heads. It cannot be so. The heart knows no logic beyond need and desire; the head has no senses except the common and the pragmatic. Neither, frankly, is useful in love anyway. Rely on your sixth sense, that little voice within. There is no preparation for or protection from the joy and pain of relationships. They are inseparable twins. One follows another. And make no mistake, love is not gay abandon; it is to be courageous, to take risks and be disciplined." ~ Ramya Varma

3 ~ The Big Copout

No expectations…no disappointment...no resentment. Not too long ago, I had an interesting conversation with one of my adult daughters. She was actually quizzing me about child rearing practices and expectations. On this particular day, she wasn't pleased with the behavior of one of her children. She mentioned that when she and her sisters were growing up, that they just knew that their father and I had expectations of them. She went on to say that she innately knew by those expectations just how far she could go. For instance, she understood that she was expected to get good grades in school, to behave in an acceptable manner whether we were there to witness it or not, to get a higher education and to excel in her efforts to be all that she could be no matter her walk in life. This daughter also told me that our having expectations of her and her sisters helped set the bar for their personal growth and success because they learned to have reasonable goals and expectations of themselves.

My husband and I have always had expectations of ourselves. We are both goal oriented and have set numerous personal and couple targets over the years. We then worked hard to attain these sometimes difficult goals, which at times, stretched not only over the span of weeks or months, but over several years. When we failed, and we did fail on more than one occasion, we just tried harder and prayed for the guidance that we needed in order to succeed. Although, the success may not have come in the form we necessarily expected, it did indeed come. This concept taught us patience, trust, and enhanced our faith to know that there was a Divine guidance in our lives that would reward our efforts in an unexpected and refreshing way. However, nonetheless, we were not disappointed in the results of those expectations regardless the outcome.

When I look at the world around me, I think it is a positive attribute to have reasonable expectations of others, especially if I have expectations of myself and my loved ones. Although, in my opinion, it is necessary to differentiate between having reasonable expectations of others and "**un**conditional love". When and if, people don't live up to our expectations, our love should not be withdrawn. We love them no matter what the circumstance. When I have expectations of others, I am actually showing that love by treating them as a peer. In fact, I am complimenting my husband, children, family, friends and maybe even the stranger on the street. I am demonstrating my love and high regard for them because I see these individuals in the same light as I see myself. To me, to not have any expectations of others is to infer that they are less than me. I do not look at my friends or others in this way.

I consider this type of behavior…having no expectations…as a method of behavior utilized to avoid disappointment. In doing so, I am setting the bar so low that the people in my life can't help but look like winners. I liken it to letting others win at a game on purpose. However, the stakes are much higher now because this is the game of life and it's a far cry from child's play. I've been there and this kind of imbalance in a relationship is not very rewarding for either party. It inevitably results in a no win situation. To expect nothing may appear admirable at first blush but under further scrutiny and analysis, it is more of a copout than anything else. Those who prefer to or choose to merely give in a relationship and never receive, is not what I would even classify as a relationship in the first place. This type of situation will only evolve into a resentful and unrewarding pseudo-relationship in the long run.

To opt for this kind of unfulfilling encounter, not only implies that I am capable of giving more to others, the underlying action implies that others are less than me because they are unwilling or unable to give. It grants me, what I consider to be, the upper hand and suggests that the people in my life are needy and I am not. It does nothing for a person's self-esteem to even hint at the idea that they may have nothing to give back, even if it is as simple as a smile to a stranger on the street. When we expect nothing of others what are we really saying? Are we intimating that we don't need them or what they have to offer? Think about it. It is not always easy to admit that we have needs.

Relationships or friendships imply an affinity, kinship, or connection to other human beings. My friends are very much equal to me and I treat them as such and expect the same from them. It is unacceptable for me to be treated as less in any of my relationships. I expect my friends to be able to count on me during both the good times and the bad. I am no more chosen to just give to them than they are chosen to just give to me. We are all meant to give and receive on this earth. These kinds of reciprocal and respectful relationships are what make up the fabric of lasting and true friendships. This is why I have chosen to have reasonable expectations of my friends. They are as capable of giving as I am. We are the same. For that, I am eternally grateful because I very much need their prayers, their love, their support, and their encouragement just as much as I hope they need mine. I would like to think that our needs are mutually acceptable, albeit, they may occur at different times in our journey. I am truly honored when they embrace the fact that they can count on me and I want to be able to count on them too as I face both the joys and sorrows that life has to offer.

It is our mutual love and respect for each other, as well as the give and take in all healthy relationships, that have made them all the more precious to me. It has also given these kinships the strength they require to stand the test of time. It would be an ideal world if we could all be in a position to only give but I know full well that it has been a humbling experience for me to admit that I need to receive as well. This humbling experience has reminded me of the necessity for more humility in my life by accepting that I too, am needy, at times. How about you? Does it bring you comfort to know that you are not alone when it comes to facing trials and tribulations? Do you avoid having expectations of others to prevent yourself from being disappointed if they don't deliver? Do you see yourself as more giving in your relationships and then fall into the trap of resenting others when they don't reciprocate your generosity? There is plenty to reflect upon when it comes to our family relationships and friendships. Please take a few moments to dwell on the answers to these questions and how they really affect you. Be honest now…remember it's just between you and your Maker.

"We all mold one another's dreams. We all hold each other's fragile hopes in our hands. We all touch others' hearts…." ~ Source Unknown.

"The sculptor will chip off all the unnecessary material to set free the angel. Nature will chip and pound us remorselessly to bring out our possibilities. She will strip us of wealth, humble our pride, humiliate our ambition, let us down from the ladder of fame, will discipline us in a thousand different ways if she can develop a little character….There is no medicine like hope, no incentive so great, and no tonic so powerful as expectation of something tomorrow." ~ Orison Swett Marden

4 ~ You Are Not Broken ~
Andrea Ayotte Cockerill

Although the memory of our first breath when we entered this world is beyond our recollection, its innocence and wonder are no less profound. You just have to look at your own or any newborn child to see the vulnerability and utter newness of when a new soul begins its journey into the experience of being a human being. When babies grow into toddlers, you can see the fearlessness of children's innate curiosity and how it propels them into following any and all of their hearts desires, which on many occasions goes against that of their mothers!

Imagine living this way as an adult, following your heart's desires with wild abandon. At some point in our childhood we go from living fearlessly, to viewing the world as unsafe. We start to realize that not all is right with the world and we may eventually internalize it as meaning that all is not right with us. At a deep level we turn from the experience of the newborn, a being of pure perfection, to feeling as if we are someone who is broken and in need of fixing. How painful it is to see ourselves in this light. We then start the process of seeing ourselves as possessing much darker traits.

Many people may not even realize that they actually think this way because it goes beyond the awareness stage. It is at a subconscious level as evidenced by the words we say to ourselves about our lives. How many times have we said, if such and such happens, then I will feel good, be happy, find joy, be worthy of love, etc.? This kind of thinking implies that at the core of our being, something is broken. We then project this brokenness onto the surface areas of our lives, our job, our bodies, our families, our communities and the list goes on. Isn't it easier to try to fix that, which is outer, than to go deep within ourselves and feel the emotion of brokenness, vulnerability and just plain not measuring up?

In my opinion, we spend so much time protecting ourselves and our spirit, trying to fix that which is truly not broken. Yes…you are not broken. There is nothing to fix. The center of your being is pure perfection and light. It is the part of you that always was and always will be. You can't lose it, damage it, abandon it, or escape the love that resides in you. You may have developed coping mechanisms along the way to protect yourself which have created layers similar to that of an onion. With compassion and faith, each of these layers can be carefully peeled away to reveal the wonder and innocence you came with when you entered into this world as pure perfection itself.

When you learn to view yourself as whole, failure won't have such a high price tag. It won't run so deep and healing won't take so long after you stumble and fall. Highs and lows would be just a part of life because the thread running through life's challenges would originate from a feeling of innate wholeness and love. I pray for this for myself, for all women and for all humankind. I pray each one of us experiences the joy of living with wild abandon like that of an innocent child.

When I was young, I was innocent and saw the world as limitless. Now that I am older, I may see the limits of this world, but my faith sees the limitlessness of God. It is this faith that allows me to spread my wings and take a chance on life. Are you willing to take that chance too….to look deep within yourself and find that childlike love and innocence that you were born with?

"We are all born for love. It is the principle of existence, and its only end." ~ Benjamin Disraeli

"Love is the emblem of eternity: it confounds all notions of time: effaces all memories of a beginning, all fear of an end." ~ Anna Louise De Stael

5 ~ He's Got the Whole World in His Hands

I am the mother of three married daughters. I have eight delightful grandchildren and still hope to be blessed with even more. I always knew that I loved my children with all my heart but I had no way of knowing until I became a grandmother that I would love my grandchildren with the same depth. Each time a grandchild is born, I feel the same thrill as when I gave birth to their mothers.

When we raise a family we all go through the trials and tribulations that come with each phase of growing up. I remember thinking to myself that after all three daughters were married and settled down, I would have a lot less to worry about and more time to merely sit back and enjoy the fun stuff. I must admit that this was one naive thought.

As my family continues to multiply I find that I actually have more to worry about, not less. Now my daughters are experiencing some of the woes of raising their children and I am well aware of almost everything that they are going through. I try my best to encourage them to "not sweat" the small stuff. I must admit though that it's not always easy to follow my own advice. One of the things I still "sweat" about is childhood illnesses especially in the younger grandchildren. The older ones can at least tell you what's wrong when they're not feeling good but the little ones can only cry about it. Is it only in my own mind or has there been an increase in childhood illnesses? When these little ones get sick, I'm so concerned in a way that brings out the worrywart in me.

It is at these times that I have to search inside and draw from the same strength I used when my daughters were young. That strength is my faith. I know that each and every child born on earth is a whole world to God. I also know that He's got the whole world in His hands. Of that, I am sure. I not only desire to trust in Him, I very much *need* to trust in Him for the benefit of all just like my daughters *need* to do so as well.

Yes indeed…it is wonderful to have been blessed with such an ever-growing family and I thank God on a daily basis. Nevertheless, I re-iterate, it is not only the family that is multiplying but also the fears and concerns that go with it. I need my faith now more than ever in order to encourage my daughters. I want to be there for them as much as possible as they face what life has to offer. I heard many years ago, that you never fully realize how much you believe in God until you have children. I couldn't agree more! We need prayers and our faith as we work through the challenges that go with raising a family. Don't you agree? What do you do when you are faced with family crises? Who do you turn to? How has your faith helped you cope with the challenges of raising a family?

"Worrying is carrying tomorrow's load with today's strength----carrying two days at once. It is moving into tomorrow ahead of time. Worrying doesn't empty tomorrow of sorrows, it empties today of strength." ~ Corrie Ten Boom

"There are many truths of which the full meaning cannot be realized until personal experience has brought it home." ~ John Stuart Mill

6 ~ The Jongleur

I have French heritage. My dad's first language was French and I married a Frenchman just like him. Now, over forty years later when I look at my husband, I can hardly believe how much he resembles my dad. Perhaps, it is only in his mannerisms but I see more. He not only looks like him if that is possible…it is how he acts…what he says and…also how he says it. I have always loved my French background, but I have never fulfilled my dream of carrying on a conversation in the French language that I love so much.

Many years ago when I was experiencing bouts of serious depression, I used to have long periods of silence. I spent a lot of hours thinking about what was happening to me…thinking about how I had arrived at this point…and thinking about what I was going to do to positively change my lot in life. One of the French words for "to think" is "jongler". When I had some of these episodes of deep thought, my husband frequently queried me about what was going on in my mind. It was more out of concern for me than anything else. He wanted to know what I was so deeply dwelling upon in order to better help me deal with these troubling thoughts.

He knew how much I loved the French language and oftentimes he would insert French words into our English conversations. He would therefore ask me what I was "jongling" about on a regular basis. His goal was to please me as well as to bring me out of that moment of despair and into our present day state of affairs. He could tell by the expression on my face that I was troubled as I was mulling over things in my mind in order to make more sense of them.

Now, almost thirty years later, I am writing about these very thoughts in an open and forthright way. In many instances, I use the voice of the "jongleur" to do so. For those of you who don't know, the "jongleur" is a French minstrel who used to make his way from town to town to entertain people in the olden days. At times, he utilized stories or music to help do this. When I write, it is done in much the same fashion. I usually incorporate much humor…many quotes… anecdotes…and personal stories to entertain my readers. I do this to make a variety of points as well as a method of sharing my personal philosophy on life.

Now that I have succeeded in sorting through my puzzling thoughts, I feel much more comfortable, not only in sharing them with my husband and my family but with others as well. I consider myself to be a present day jongleur as I share my written musings with you. I sincerely hope that you find pleasure in getting to know me better and that you derive some benefit from my writing and what I have to say. The point to my inspirational writing is not about wanting to say something; it's more about my actual ***need*** to say it. Do you feel the ***need*** to say something that is going on in your life? Are you being an effective communicator and getting the meaning of your words and feelings across to those who care about you? In order to establish deeper and more intimate relationships, we must endeavor to become more proficient communicators. Once again, I ask. Are you readily and honestly getting your messages across to those you love and care for? Are you being true to yourself?

"We must become acquainted with our emotional household; we must see our feelings as they actually are. This breaks their hypnotic and damaging hold on us." ~ *Vernon Howard*

7 ~ The Three R's

For those of you who have read my background information in the Introduction, you already know that I am a former elementary school teacher. During my teaching years, I spent a great deal of time teaching the three R's of education; that of, *r*eading, *r*iting and *r*ithmetic as they were so fondly called in those days.

Today we are utilizing many other words that start with the letter R such as recycle, reuse, and restore in an effort to be energy conscious and to help protect and sustain our environment.

Although, I left the classroom many years ago, the classroom has never left me. Once a teacher, always a teacher! It's in my blood. In fact, my other published books are what I consider to be teaching tools. My words are never meant to offend but rather, to educate.

The reason I have chosen to discuss the three R's of education is pretty straightforward. Other than the ones I have already mentioned in the first two paragraphs, there are many more equally important words starting with the letter R.

A few of these are responsibility, respect, and reciprocity/relationship building. When people hold themselves accountable for their actions, they demonstrate a sense of responsibility. Consequently, when they become more accountable and accept responsibility, these individuals develop self-respect and in turn earn the respect of others. By earning the respect of others, this concept eventually results in a mutually respectful relationship. This is what I refer to as the beginnings of a reciprocal connection or affinity. Simply put, what goes around comes around.

As I whisper now to you...whether positive or negative, people eventually become the reflection of each other. In other words, those around you will be a reflection of yourself and your values. How is your reflection in the mirror looking back at you? Do you like what you see? Usually the people around us are the most similar to us because like-minded individuals have the tendency to gravitate toward each other. Do you like and enjoy those around you? If not, why? If so, you might very well ask yourself the same thing in order to get a better picture of who you are and what you're all about. I re-iterate...do you like what you see? Trust me this is a very important question but not nearly as important as your answer.

"As human beings we are endowed with freedom of choice, and we can not shuffle off our responsibility upon

the shoulders of God or nature. We must shoulder it ourselves. It is up to us." ~ Arnold J. Toynbee

8 ~ Confidence in God

Have you ever been given a precious gift with very little monetary value that means so much to you? Many years ago, long before my father passed away, he gave each of his children a booklet titled "Confidence in God ~ Words of Encouragement" by Rev. Daniel Considine S. J. It is very small, about 3" by 5"…and has 94 pages. What I didn't realize at the time was quite how dear this little gift meant to me. I thoroughly enjoyed reading it and have done so on numerous occasions since. Unfortunately, I no longer have the original booklet. I merely have a copy that I purchased at a later date. What actually made the first one so very special to me was my father's signature inside…to my daughter Dolores…love Dad.

Upon receiving this token of love, I was so thrilled with its content that I shared this booklet with the mother of one of the students I was teaching at the time. I wanted to pass along its beautiful message. I soon regretted my decision but it was too late to do anything about it. I now wish I had kept that original little gift from my father and just given away one of the new booklets that I purchased at a later date but it was after the fact. The original booklet soon became so priceless to me, yet I had parted with it without a moment's thought or the slightest hesitation. I eventually purchased several more of these very booklets and gave them away as delightful little gifts myself.

The content remains the same and although the message in it is very dear to me and still holds true today, my replacement booklet does not have that personal inscription from my father. I miss him and the special touch of his loving words that have come to mean so much to me over the years. Today I am much more sentimental. Years ago, in my haste and with the right intentions, I gave away a gift that cannot be replaced. Every time I read my copy of "Confidence in God" I think of my Dad and I long to see his signature inside. Have you ever done that? Have you ever given away some priceless, little gift that cannot be replaced no matter how hard you try?

I want to share a quote with you from this booklet. When I randomly opened the pages, this was the first one to jump out at me. ***"It is no small penance in these days merely to bear with yourself; and if you bear properly with yourself and your neighbor, God will give you the highest graces."*** I would have to say that this is the message that God would like us to hear today.

Yes…merely to bear properly with yourself and your neighbor. So much easier said than done, don't you think?

Please think about this today as you make your way on whatever path lays ahead for you. Just for today…tomorrow will come soon enough.

"God does not require you to follow His leading on blind trust. Behold the evidence of an invisible intelligence pervading everything, even your own mind and body." ~ *Raymond Holliwell*

9 ~ First Things First

"From our childhood many of us have been told more of the punishments God has in store for us if we fail to please Him than the rewards He looks forward to giving when we do please Him....The first thing in loving our Lord is to believe Him lovable. What are the sorts of persons one loves? First, they must be easy to get on with. How many in their heart of hearts think our Lord easy to get on with? We think Him touchy, unapproachable, easily annoyed or offended. And yet all this fear of Him pains Him very much. Would our father wish us to hang our heads, be shy and shrinking in his presence? How much less so our Heavenly Father? He has an almost foolish love for us." **(Rev. Daniel Considine in "Confidence in God~Words of Encouragement")**

How many of you can relate to this quote? How many of you can think back to your childhood and remember the fear that was instilled in you? How many of you remember hearing about the fires of eternal damnation and that you would burn there if you didn't do what God wanted? Yes…we learned full well the punishments of God!

On the other hand, how many of you, in your early childhood, ever heard that God loved you? I, for one, didn't.

In all the teachings I learned as a child, I never once recall hearing the word *Love* to describe how God felt about me or anyone else for that matter. If you are in my age bracket, the word God and *Love* never went hand in hand. The word reward was never heard either. The word punishment definitely was used to describe what God was all about and what His plans for us would be if we didn't toe the line. How much damage was done to some of the children of my era? Are you one of them?

I think Rev. Daniel Considine has it right. It took me twenty-five years to write *I'm Not Perfect & It's Okay*. It's hard to believe it took me that long to put pen to paper and write my first book. In actuality, it took me that long to garner the courage and determination to set the record straight. God loves me, warts and all and He loves you too!

Take a moment to reflect on all the little ways God shows His *Love* for you. At times, we are so busy with are lives that we miss what is "hiding in plain sight". Yes…please just take a moment to be grateful for your life.

"The cure for all the ills and wrongs, the cares, the sorrows, and the crimes of humanity, all lie in that one word 'love'. It is the divine vitality that everywhere produces and restores life." ~ Lydia Maria Child

10 ~ Psst...Hey EWE!

Yes you! Now that I've caught your attention I really want to talk to you. By chance, do you enjoy doing Crosswords and other types of puzzles? If so, this is the chapter for you.

Ever since I can remember, I have been a puzzle solver. I truly love the mental challenge of trying to figure things out. It is unbelievable how mentally stimulating and life enriching these puzzles can be. In most local newspapers, there is a wealth of knowledge at our fingertips just ready to be tapped into on a daily basis.

Now why did I choose the word EWE in my title to get your attention? Most of you probably know that EWE is another word for a female sheep. Over and over again this word comes up in Crossword Puzzles. Every time I see it when solving a puzzle, it reminds me of Jesus Christ and how He is described as the gentle Lamb. If we are to emulate Christ and follow in His footsteps we, too, must be like gentle lambs in our dealings with people.

As we all know, it is not always easy to be gentle and kind. Many times in life, our patience is tested as we become frustrated with the people around us. In some instances, people may be unaware of this fact but on other occasions we may only be fooling ourselves into thinking that they don't take notice of exactly how we feel. The tone of our voice and our body language can quickly give away our true feelings despite what our words may say.

I find as I do my daily Crossword Puzzle that God works in mysterious ways. I hear God's Word many times as I solve these puzzles. I can do an examination of conscience and ask myself if I have had any cross...words with any one in my life. God can prompt me on several occasions throughout these puzzles if I am open to His cues/clues. He reminds me to emulate the gentle Lamb that so aptly demonstrates a mother's love. In doing so, it gives me the desire to follow in His footsteps when I come across the word EWE.

Other times, one of the clues will ask for the letters found on the cross. Yes...INRI. Again, I am reminded that the Lamb died on the cross for the salvation of humankind. This inscription reinforces the fact that I have sinned and Jesus' forgiveness is so great that He chose to die on the cross to save my soul and yours too. He is the Teacher and I am the student. Frequently, I need to be reminded to be ready to forgive at all times because my transgressions have so generously been forgiven.

It is truly amazing to see the many creative ways that God can reach out to people. God has a way of utilizing all of His followers and reminding them of their mission in life. We only need to be open to hearing the message whenever and wherever it presents itself.

God is very creative indeed. He knows our regular haunts and just when and how to reach us in order to get His worthwhile message across. I much prefer Crosswords to cross…words, if EWE know what I mean. How about you? Have you said some angry words lately that you aren't feeling too good about…or has someone offended you by their harsh words? As challenging and enjoyable as solving Crossword puzzles may be, we all know that it is far harder to solve the dilemmas created by our cross words with others. Yes…we have all been there whether on the giving end or the receiving end. Most often, we struggle with solving this type of problem and could use a Higher Power to guide us. Wouldn't you agree?

"The very greatest things…great thoughts, discoveries, inventions…have usually been nurtured in hardship, often pondered over in sorrow, and at length established with difficulty." ~ Samuel Smiles

11 ~ The Absence Of

I know...you're never supposed to end a sentence with a preposition, but perhaps I can make an exception in this case because I have merely ended a title with one. I find that when I write, I take a few creative liberties and bend some of the grammatical rules as I see fit. Some fellow authors may very well choose to do the same. I hope so because as liberal minded as I may think I am, it always feels good to know that I am not totally alone with any particular point of view.

Today, I am about to express one of those views. The other day, I read a neat email sent to me by a long time Christian friend. This article really got me thinking about some of my own "isms". The theme of the article had to do with opinions on science versus the existence of God. I'm not going to go on and on about what I read because I want to zero in on what captured my attention the most.

First of all, it was the concept of the description of death as the "absence of life". The article mentioned that you cannot scientifically measure death so therefore, death should be referred to as the "absence of life". This concept is quite clear and easily understood. As I continued to read, it was obvious to me that this article was fast becoming more philosophical than scientific because God was described as the Light, while evil was described as the "absence of Light". In other words, those of us without God in our lives would be living in darkness. I'm pretty sure we have all heard this phrase before to describe different aspects of Christian faith or lack of it.

As a result of some introspection, this concept made me look at my faith from another angle. It reminded me of the story about Jesus fishing in the stormy waters with His disciples. When they kept their eyes on Him, the apostles had faith and knew no fear. They were unafraid of the dark skies and the turbulent waters surrounding them and the imminent risk they posed. However, the exact opposite happened when they lost their focus and stopped looking at Jesus. Perhaps, the same theory holds true for us. The "absence of faith" results in fear. When we are afraid, when we feel fear…is it because we really have something to fear or is it because we have taken our eyes off of Jesus? Do we give the concept of fear "life" and let it have power over us and what we choose to do or not do?

It is very difficult to overcome fear. I try my best to remember what Jesus taught us about perfect love casting out fear. Jesus offers His perfect, unconditional love. I do not want to be afraid. I want to know, love and serve the Lord with a deep abiding faith with the "absence of fear". When I feel fear, it seems that I have done the exact opposite. I have taken my eyes off of Jesus and I experience the "absence of faith". I much prefer to have it the other way around. I also need to remind myself that the word "fear" can mean "to be in awe" or "to have reverence and respect" in some instances.

My relationship with God is one of those instances. I have every desire to be in "awe" of the God who created me out of love rather than to be afraid of making mistakes and fearing His retribution for my human weaknesses.

I do not want to live with the impression that I am constantly being judged by my Creator who is ready to punish me if I take a wrong turn. For in reality, He wants to show me nothing but His infinite love and mercy, not only for me, but for all His creatures. I once "feared" God but in all honestly is was the wrong kind of "fear". I "feared" punishment and retribution rather than being in "awe" of the loving Father that I now readily embrace. How do you view God? Are you afraid? Do you act out of true love and a desire to please our Maker or do you do the right thing for the wrong reason. "Fear" of being punished? I gently ask you to think about it...really think about it. Your answer may very well surprise you. There is such a fine line to walk and it's very easy to mix up the two emotions.

"Most of our obstacles would melt away if, instead of cowering before them, we should make up our minds to walk boldly through them." ~ *Orison Swett Marden*

12 ~ Love Triangle ~ Fred Ayotte

I know many of you have heard of a love triangle where two people love the same person. In this situation, the two suitors usually don't like each other at all. This happened to me during my thirties and forties with my wonderful wife.

In my late thirties, on the thirteenth birthday of one of my twin daughters, she acquired a brownish-red, miniature poodle named Joey. He was a very beautiful dog. However, as time went by in our house, Joey came to believe that he and my wife were the married couple and that I was the odd man out.

Many times I had to set him straight. For instance, my wife always went to bed a few hours earlier than me. At that time, Joey would jump onto the bed and sleep on my side of the bed. When I retired later, he did not want to move. I had to physically remove him (very gently) and put him on the floor so that I could get into my side of the bed. There were many other similar events like this where he thought I was the third wheel in our house and I had to set him straight yet again. Needless to say, I was not a big fan of his and he wanted very little to do with me on several occasions.

Many years later, when my daughter eventually got her own place, she took Joey with her. Well, as you know, dogs do not have as long a life span as humans. In his thirteenth year, Joey became quite sick. After numerous trips to the vet, we knew it was just a matter of time until he would have to be put down in order to prevent him from needless suffering.

A few days before he passed away, we just so happened to be visiting at our daughter's apartment. I was sitting on a chair when Joey came right up to me and just sat on his haunches right at my feet. I automatically reached down to pick him up and he didn't put up a fuss like he normally did. He just sat on my lap very quietly without even trying to move or get down.

A few days later he passed away. I know, even if no one else believes me that Joey came to me before he died so we could make amends for our relationship. In his own way he was forgiving me for my behavior or asking me to forgive him. I will never know for sure but either way was fine with me. It's too bad, we as humans; oftentimes, can't or won't be anywhere near as forgiving as Joey. What a wonderful world this would be if we were. What do you think? Is there something to be learned from our animal friends? Do you need to reach out and forgive someone or perhaps you are in need of forgiveness today?

"Friendship is the only cement that will ever hold the world together." ~ Woodrow Wilson

13 ~ Positive Attitude

I recall going bowling a few times in my younger years. To be honest, I do not have an athletic bone in my body. This one time, I got the worst score possible. It was so embarrassing! The bowling alley was full of fun-loving people and I didn't even realize that anyone had been watching me until after the game. This older gentleman came up to me and introduced himself as a minister.

He said something which has stuck in my mind all these years... something that I didn't even realize I was doing because it came so naturally to me. Obviously he could see how badly I was bowling. It was pretty apparent to everyone in or around the vicinity. He proceeded to tell me that after every ball I threw, no matter how bad it was, I would turn around and smile at my fellow bowlers. He then told me how wonderful he thought this was. *Wow...it was like, how could anyone smile after bowling the way that I did!* I was so grateful for the compliment that I thanked him and then gave him one of my biggest smiles. It meant the world to me that someone had given me such a fine a compliment. That's me in a nutshell, forever the smiley one...forever the eternal optimist. You know the one...the one, who would be searching for a dog if she found a pile of dung in the garage while someone else would be cursing the mess. I would think that someone probably gave me a new puppy as a gift and I would be busy trying to find it. There could be no other explanation! Right?

You want to know my secret? I can usually find the bright side to just about anything. This has been my saving grace in facing the many ups and downs of daily living. It has been said that *"it is worth a thousand dollars a year to have the habit of looking on the bright side of things"*. ~ *Orville Gilbert Brim* So in other words, it is probably where some of my greatest wealth lies because in most instances this is exactly how I choose to view life. Choose is the key word here. In life we have many choices and our attitude usually has a huge impact on how we view life. I guess you could always ask yourself if you see your *"glass as half empty or half full"*. Your answer might give you a better understanding of what I mean. Do you consider yourself to have a positive attitude? If so, is this actually the image you are portraying?

I have a little line I use with my husband now and then. When someone tells me they are happy but I just can't tell by their expression, I say that perhaps, "they should tell their face". Do you have a down-at-the-mouth expression, lifeless eyes, or a chip on your shoulder? If you do, I can guarantee that your face shows it. Check it out and see for yourself. Take a moment to smile in the mirror and see if your eyes light up with joy. Do they? Do you want an instant, cost free face lift...if so, all you need to do is smile as often as possible. I guarantee you that it will take years off your face. I have observed this phenomenon for a very long time. Perhaps, you should just start there. See for yourself by observing the smiles on the faces of those around you. I certainly wish you could tell me the results of this little experiment...but then, what matters most is that you take me at my word and check it out for yourself.

"The greatest discovery of my generation is that human beings can alter their lives by altering their attitudes of mind." ~ William James

"The greatest power that a person possesses is the power to choose" ~ J. Martin Kohe

14 ~ The Truth

The truth..."*It may not lead you to where you thought you were going, but it will always lead you somewhere better. When ignored, it will eventually show itself. The closeness of your relationships is directly proportional to the degree to which you have revealed the truth about yourself. It can be painful*". ~ Source Unknown

It is not always easy to have honest and open relationships. The more honest the relationship, the more vulnerable we become...it is one of the reasons that we choose to wear masks in life. We do this to protect ourselves from what others may think or say about us. We usually try to put our best foot forward in order to impress people. The more comfortable we become in a relationship, the more we feel safe to take down these barriers.

The truth... "*It's a process of peeling away the layers of your false self, your trying-to-be-something-you're-not self, your copycat self, your trying-to-sound-a-certain-way self, your spent-my-life-watching-television self. It's like going to psychotherapy, delving deep and allowing the real* *you to emerge; only in this case you want it to find its way on to the page."* ~ Rachelle Gardner

Yes, **the truth** may not lead you to where you thought you were going but would you want it any other way?

The truth…if and when you choose to embrace it, has a way of cleansing your soul like a pleasant rain that falls ever so gently and washes away all your weaknesses.

The truth…gives us the courage to face all that life offers.

The truth…if you are an author, is why we have chosen to write and to bare our souls to those who honor us by reading our words. Yes, **the truth** for those who seek it, can find its way to the page. May you feel the mist on your face that mingles with your tears as you wash away your woes when you…humbly and sincerely…discover the truth in your life. I don't mean **your** truth…I mean **the** truth. There is a definite and distinctive difference in the way we perceive things and the way that they actually are.

Please take a moment to reflect on this truism. Do you know the truth about your life, your actions, the motive behind those actions and what it means to have the strength and courage to face the reality of your choices? Merely respond with the plain truth and no prettying up of the facts. In all honesty, it is never easy to really face the facts and the part we may have played in any given situation.

"Reality isn't the way you wish things to be, nor the way they appear to be, but the way they actually are." ~ Robert J. Ringer

15 ~ On Being Judgmental

Once again, I had an interesting conversation with one of my daughters a short time ago. In this conversation, she used the word 'judgmental' as a negative or undesirable trait. She mentioned during this conversation that she did not want to be a 'judgmental' person. I have also heard other people say such statements as "I'm tired of being judged". I find the use of this word rather foreign to me. I personally, seldom if ever, feel like I am being judged by others. Perhaps, some people do judge me and I just don't recognize it. Therefore, I can't honestly say for sure whether I have been judged in the past or not. However, as an author, I find that it is necessary for me to have a wide variety of opinions. It would be pretty difficult to write books, articles, or blogs without having them.

I know that I am not the only one with observational skills and personal opinions. I also know that it is required in all walks of life in order to be able to accurately assess situations and people. Oftentimes this habit results in making more informed decisions. As the years go by, I find that I am better able to analyze what I am observing and where these observations will lead me. It would seem that this skill is enhanced by a combination of age plus experience. At this time, in order to better make my point, I am going to get a little philosophical and use an analogy to better explain my assessment of the use of the word 'judgmental'.

Many years ago when I suffered from depression, which is considered to be a form of mental illness, I was ashamed about my condition and chose to hide this fact from my family and friends as much as possible. I felt that there was a "stigma" attached to mental illness and I did not want anyone to know. Therefore, I kept it a well-hidden secret except from my husband and my parents. Even so, they never knew the full extent of my suffering or despair. I managed to hide it from them to varying degrees as well. Now, after almost thirty years, I am able to not only write about my experiences but if the appropriate opportunity arises, I am far more willing to discuss what I went through.

The conclusion I arrived at after all these years, is that I actually had a bias myself. I know it was a learned bias based on my personal frame of reference, but it was a bias nonetheless. At the time of my illness, I was projecting how I thought society in general, viewed mental illness when I was the one actually thinking it. Does that make sense? If I didn't have my own bias toward mental illness, I would have been far more open and forthright about it in the first place regardless of what anyone thought. Are you still with me here?

Okay, now I want to return to the concept of 'being judgmental' or the feeling of 'being judged'. I think the same rationale I used for admitting to my own prejudice also applies here. Perhaps, people who sense that they are being judged have that trait in their own personality. If they think they are being judged in any way, shape, or form, maybe it is because they are actually judgmental towards others themselves. If a trait is part of our own character make up, we might assume that others share this same trait as well. Does this make sense to you?

We can and do project the emotions that we are dealing with on others. We actually have no idea what other people are thinking. If we choose to express our views on other people's thoughts, we are only sharing what is going on in our own minds and assuming that they think the same way. What I'm basically trying to say is this. What we think we see in others may actually live within ourselves. The only way we can ever really know what someone else is thinking is if or when they decide to share their thoughts with us. Also, it is a well-known adage that the very things we don't like about others are what we actually don't like about ourselves. Is this ideology familiar to you? If so, perhaps, it's time to have a better look about *why* we dislike certain individuals and *what* we can do about it. A better understanding of ourselves often leads to a better understanding and acceptance of those around us.

"We are only falsehood, duplicity, contradiction; we both conceal and disguise ourselves from ourselves." ~ *Blaise Pascal*

"A clear understanding of negative emotions dismisses them." ~ *Vernon Howard*

16 ~ Connecting the Dots

When you were a young child, did you ever have the opportunity to do "connect the dot" pictures in your activity/coloring book? I know they still have these enjoyable little learning tools today as I've seen my children and now my grandchildren receive the same pleasure that I did as a young child when engaging in this type of fun. After joining the numbers or connecting the dots, they too, can see the picture and then color it in.

In life, I envision God's Plan as much the same. From my point of view, it's similar to a bunch of dots which are in the processing of being connected so that His Divine Plan or picture will eventually be revealed to us as humankind. Over the last several weeks and months, I have touched base with many fellow authors and have had the opportunity to feel very connected to these gifted people. One referred to this experience as a "God thing"…another referred to it as a "God connection". As to be expected, it feels wonderful to connect with other like-minded individuals in the atmosphere of love, acceptance, and co-operation. I personally refer to it as connecting the dots, with the dots actually being the people in our lives. This opportunity helps to further unveil what God has in store for us as we work together toward achieving a common goal. When these moments occur, I can tell you that it feels so right, just like when we were children and we finished our "dot-to-dot" picture. Although just like when we were young, we might occasionally connect the wrong dots in the picture. As adults, we may also connect the wrong dot in our dealings with people. At these times, it usually doesn't look or feel right. There's kind of a niggling inside of us that just won't leave us alone. At that point, we have to make a mental decision to retrace our steps and erase where we erred in order to get back on track. Does this ever happen to you? Are there some people in your life that you are not comfortable with and that you know you shouldn't have a relationship with them…or a least not at the present time?

At times, we can connect with a person whom at first blush appears to be a "dot" or a "God connection". After a while though, their behavior may change. Instead of working together for the common good, our relationship takes a negative turn. We might become unexpected competitors resulting in feelings of disappointment and resentment. These "friends" may start putting us down or taking what they require from us in order to succeed or further their own agenda. In the great scheme of things, if and when, we are striving to do God's Will here on earth, we are not competitors vying for some golden cup. The key is to help, support, and encourage each other because the prize is the same for us all.

When we don't positively or productively connect with people, we are not working toward the completion of God's Big Picture. This, in reality is supposed to be the common goal. We need each other. Are you a "dot" working toward the common goal or do you have your own personal agenda? What about those closest to you? Do you have your eyes on the same end result or are you wasting a lot of time and energy working against each other? Negative energy can be non-productive, very exhausting, and a total waste of precious time. I think the following quote sums it up pretty well.

"What I do you cannot do; but what you do, I cannot do. The needs are great, and none of us, including me, ever do great things. But we can all do small things, with great love, and together we can do something wonderful." ~ **Cindie Thomas**

17 ~ Child's Play...or is it?

I want to tell you a cute little story with a very big lesson in it. When I was a very young girl about six years old or so, I spent a great deal of time playing with the neighborhood kids. In those days, you could go freely from one house to the next without a lot of concern by your parents. One day a little girl named Yvette, asked me to come over and play dolls at her house. She was a bit younger than me but I was happy to play with her just the same. Right at the onset, she told me that she had already called on two other little girls (sisters) but they were having their afternoon nap. They actually did that in those days too, right up until you started school.

Yvette and I played for a least an hour in her back porch with her mother periodically checking up on us. We both had a wonderful time. Shortly thereafter, there was a knock on the door and there appeared the two sisters that Yvette originally wanted to play with. In they came and with that...out I went. Yvette promptly told me that I had to go home because now they could play with her and that was her original plan. As I mentioned earlier, she told me right up front that she had called on them first. I never gave it a moment's thought and I just got up and quietly left.

Within what felt like only a few minutes, Yvette came running down the sidewalk and asked me to come back and play. She explained to me that her mother came out to check on us and she discovered that I wasn't there anymore. From what I could gather, her mother asked where I was and Yvette admitted to her that she had sent me home. Her mother went on to say that it wasn't a kind thing to do. She then encouraged Yvette to go find me and invite me back to play dolls with her and the other two little girls. Her mother apparently saw no reason why the four of us couldn't just play together and neither did I. I quickly accepted her request and returned to Yvette's house. Her mother then treated us all to Popsicles.

I will never forget this incident as long as I live. Yvette is not the only one that learned a valuable lesson that day because I know something very much resonated with me. I don't know how many times I see adults treat their friends this exact same way except they are no longer at child's play. When someone else comes along, they might have the tendency to drop the friends they have and move on…or they have some kind of pecking list when it comes to the order of their friends. If their first choice is unavailable, they will simple go down their mental list in order to find someone who is free. Every time I see such unacceptable behavior I think of Yvette's mom. I wish she had been there for these people when they were young children so that they would know how to treat people in their adult life.

I've been told that we learn all we need to know as far as how we are supposed to treat others by the time we are in kindergarten. It doesn't hurt to remind ourselves of these little lessons so that we can treat our adult friends with the love and respect that they deserve. Good for Yvette's mom for taking the time to make a difference in her daughter's life, the lives of the other two little girls and mine as well. She will never fully know how much that act of kindness meant to me that memorable day so many years ago. Mothers have a very important job…in fact it may very well be the most instrumental and influential one in forming the values of our children. It is a wise thing to acknowledge this fact because mothers are the very first teachers in their children's lives. Do you remember any special childhood lessons? Do you still try to keep them in mind in your adult life? Treating people with love and respect never changes no matter what our age. Do unto others…yup, it's still applies today. Morals and values never go out of style.

"Only mothers can think of the future…because they give birth to it in their children." ~ Maxim Gorky

"There is no greater religion than human service. To work for the common good is the greatest creed." ~ *Albert Schweitzer*

"Life is a succession of lessons which must be lived to be understood." ~ *Ralph Waldo Emerson*

18 ~ Found Money

A strange thing happened to me on my morning walk. I usually walk two miles every morning with my husband but today he was off mowing our daughter's lawn. I decided to stick my ear plugs in and enjoy some music as I walked alone. I met a few people on my path. One was a jogger, another was a biker, and the final one was a mother with two young boys. As I walked along enjoying the music, I spotted a sealed envelope on the grassy boulevard that obviously all three of these people had missed. Initially, I thought someone had dropped a piece of mail so I picked it up and thought I would just pop it in the mail box for them. On closer inspection, I could see through the transparent window of the envelope that there was cash inside because I could see a $50 bill. On the front of it was written the name Gina ($200).

I have found money before but it is usually in the form of coins. I have also found the odd paper money but never have I found $200. About 30 years ago I found a $1 bill that has "Jesus Loves You" written on it and I still have it folded up in my wallet to this day. When I find this kind of money, it feels good. However, finding this $200 did not feel good at all. It reminded me of when my teenage daughter had a paper route. She was supposed to go shopping after school but when she used the rest room, she accidentally forgot her cash in an envelope by the sink. There was $100 in it and she was absolutely heartsick when she went to check at the lost and found and discovered that no one had turned it in. We helped her out by giving her some money but she has never forgotten that moment and neither have I.

Today when I found this cash, in my mind I saw the face of my heartsick daughter. Although I had no idea who Gina was or what she looked like, I knew in my heart I wanted to make an earnest effort to find her. I never opened the envelope nor did I put it in my pocket. I hoped someone would see me carrying it and claim it. I held the envelope in my hand visible for all to see just in case I passed by the owner of this cash. I kept my eyes open for someone who might be searching for it. As I backtracked, I ran into the woman with the young boys but now she was alone. She was going in the opposite direction with her back to me and I could see that she was on the phone. She didn't seem to be looking for a lost envelope but I decided to call out to her anyways...I yelled out "hi".

When she turned around, I asked if her name was Gina and she said "no". I was about to continue on my way when she called back to me. She then asked why I was looking for Gina because she knew her. She informed me that Gina was her children's babysitter. I explained that I had found an envelope with Gina's name on it. That's all, no more information than that. She then started to walk toward me. She looked so relieved as she told me that the envelope contained $200 and it fell out of the boys' lunch kit while they were walking to Gina's earlier in the morning. This is when I first encountered her. If you would have seen the look on this young mother's face. I think it was sheer disbelief bordering on shock when I handed her the sealed envelope with the $200 still in it. I may have made her day but you know something, she made mine too. It felt so rewarding to find her and give back what wasn't mine in the first place.

    A very similar situation occurred a few years ago when my husband and I were at a very crowded flea market in Mesa, AZ. A young couple was walking ahead of us. The young man had his hands in his pockets and when he pulled one hand out, a big wad of money fell to the ground behind him. He was totally oblivious as my husband bent down to pick it up. My husband could have simply put it in his pocket or…we could have easily turned down an aisle or walked into a kiosk and went along our merry way. The couple just kept walking ahead of us until my husband tapped the fellow on the shoulder and said "You dropped your money". Seeing both their faces was priceless. They were totally speechless and obviously unbelievably grateful as shown by their shocked expressions. I know there's an old saying that goes like this "a fool and his money are soon parted" but in this case we were very willing to part with this found money. Neither my husband nor I are fools. It was not our money in either instance and we took great pleasure in returning it to the rightful owners. I wish someone had done that with my daughter all those years ago. Being honest gives us the opportunity to have more faith in humankind.

Take a moment to reflect upon some of your personal experiences or your own acts of kindness and how they made you feel…or reflect on a memory of an act of kindness bestowed upon you. Sometimes, the smallest act of kindness can have the most profound effect. Does it ever feel genuinely good to keep something that isn't rightfully yours? Is it not far more rewarding to exemplify the traits of honesty and integrity? To be sure, it is a fine example to set for others, especially our children and definitely a desirable behavior to emulate.

"You can never lose anything that really belongs to you, and you can't keep that which belongs to someone else." ~ Edgar Cayce

19 ~ Drip...Drop ~ A Christmas Thought

When we think about erosion in our environment, we may picture a huge wave beating against the wall of a cliff at sea. Eventually as it pounds away, the cliff caves in and the waves continue to erode the shore line.

In many of our personal relationships, the erosion that takes place doesn't always occur in the same dramatic way. Sometimes, it does take one big upset similar to a tsunami to end a relationship but usually it takes many years of neglect or even physical or emotional abuse. At times, our unacceptable or unattractive behavior is more subtle, like a lack of consideration or unkind behavior to those around us as the drip...drop of our uncaring ways eat away at the bond we may have once shared. The drip....drop may include gossip or maligning another person's reputation. The drip...drop may also include conditional love which is the act of forcing others to earn our love by their behavior.

Whether with family or friends, a continuous drip...drop of inappropriate behavior eventually takes its toll and the relationship caves in much like the major erosion previously described. To create and maintain a quality relationship, it is necessary to show that we care. We do this by taking the time to cultivate or maintain these special connections. In doing so, it is essential to put forth the much-needed effort in order to keep the relationship alive and healthy. In my opinion, if we don't do this, the relationship will not be very positive nor very rewarding. More than likely it will eventually die.

Caring about the people we love involves making them feel like a special part of our lives. It's not about taking them for granted but rather about showing our appreciation and love for them in some of the simplest ways…putting them first on the list instead of last, a special card, a visit…or any other small act of kindness that we may choose in order to let our family or friends know we love them.

Please, during this special Christmas Season as we celebrate the birth of Jesus, it is wise to remind ourselves to make room in the "Inn" of our hearts instead of allowing the drip…drop…of our behavior to force our family and friends into the stable of our lives. If that's where they are…perhaps we must ask ourselves why. Have we really and honestly made room at our "Inn" or have we made them feel like they belong outside? Having room at our "Inn" is a year-long activity not a once a year occasion.

Hopefully, the true meaning of Christmas and the celebration of Christ's birth will also be exemplified by our behavior between New Year's and Christmas, rather than the short week between Christmas and New Year's. In order to celebrate a wondrous, peaceful, and joyous Christ-filled Christmas, as well as an abundant year, it is necessary to make room in our "Inn" all year long! Is your Christmas Season one week long or do you celebrate the birth of Christ in your heart the other fifty-one weeks of the year?

"I am convinced that the world is not a mere bog in which men and women trample themselves in the mire and die. Something magnificent is taking place here amid the cruelties and tragedies, and the supreme challenge to intelligence is that of making the noblest and best in our curious heritage." ~ Charles A. Beard

20 ~ Christmas Love

The Christmas Season is upon us once again. It is only two short weeks until Christmas Eve. The hustle and bustle of Christmas is all around us as we hurry and scurry about to finish our shopping and plan for all the usual celebrations. I want to draw from some precious memories to stress the importance of keeping the true meaning of Christmas alive as we come to the end of another year. In order to do so, I am going to travel back into my own childhood and the memories that I cherish from so long ago.

When I was a young girl, Christmas was seldom about giving gifts. If I received one…it was usually an unwrapped and much-needed article. I considered myself blessed to receive any present at all. The excitement mounted in our home regardless of the lack of presents. Christmas Eve was the start of the family celebratory season with a midnight church service followed by the special treats of homemade "tortiere"/ meat pie and other Christmas delights.

My siblings and I would tie our stockings to our wrought iron bed and wait for morning with eager anticipation. Sometime during the night, my dad would creep into our bedroom and quietly put one Christmas orange, a few unshelled peanuts, and some hard unwrapped candy at the bottom of our long stockings...stockings that we actually wore and only used in this manner once a year for this special occasion. Even when we were very young, we never talked about Santa Claus. We seemed to always know that it was my Dad putting those few items in our stockings for which we were ever so grateful to receive.

To me, Christmas Love is really about family but even more importantly, it is about celebrating the birth of Christ. In doing so, we are sharing in the joy of the holy family of Jesus, Mary, and Joseph and that special birth of Our Savior that took place over 2000 years ago.

At times, it is apparent to me that society has taken the Christ out of Xmas and replaced it with many un-Christ-like substitutes...a multitude of X's. There is much Xtravagance, many unrealistic Xpectations, too much Xtra spending, Xaggerated gift giving, Xcessive eating, Xhaustion, and too many other Xmas activities to mention. In order to truly experience the meaning of Christmas Love, it is necessary to get back to basics and keep Christ in our Christmas festivities by removing as many X's as possible.

I also feel it is necessary to refocus and redefine what Christmas is all about and what we can personally do to recapture some of the love, joy, and peace of this wondrous season.

Is your Christmas Season filled...*less* with the Xploits of consumerism and...*more* with the Love of Christ? This is what Christmas Love is all about and why I think it is so precious. Wouldn't you agree?

"The cure for all the ills and wrongs, the cares, the sorrows, and the crimes of humanity, all lie in that one word "love'. It is the divine vitality that everywhere produces and restores life." ~ **Lydia Maria Child**

Conclusion

I hope you have enjoyed my compilation of inspirational quotes and anecdotes. The main source of my quotes is from the book titled, "The Best of Success ~ A Treasury of Ideas" compiled by Wynn Davis. This book is a lovely present that my husband and I received many years ago. As you can well imagine, it is a much cherished and well used gift. I truly love and appreciate the wisdom of others and have personally benefited from the wealth of knowledge that is found in their inspirational words.

"A Woman's Voice" ~ Volume I ~ is my voice reaching out to each of you in a soft and caring manner. These are a series of short stories adopted and edited from my blogsite also titled, "A Woman's Voice". The only exceptions are the two touching stories provided by my husband, Fred, and my daughter, Andrea. My goal in all of my written words is to touch your heart and soul in such a way that you might know true peace and inner joy no matter the circumstance. Peace and joy....beyond human understanding is one of my greatest hopes for each of you.

Please watch for "A Woman's Voice" ~ Volume II. I have every desire to share my thoughts and experiences with you. May God grant you His choicest blessings in all that you say and do. Please know that He is the strength found during our weakest moments in life. I have come to the profound realization that it has been well worth being weak...in order to recognize and embrace that Divine strength. I wouldn't want it any other way!

SAMPLE CHAPTER

A Woman's Voice ~ Volume 2

17 ~ Having a Bad Day

"Take each day and relish each moment. Take each bad day and work to make it good." ~ Lisa Dado

"If you get a second chance, grab it with both hands. If it changes your life, let it. Nobody said life would be easy, they just promised it would be worth it." ~ Source Unknown

I want to share a cute little story with you to demonstrate how simple it is to turn your life around one step at a time. Many years ago when I was working downtown in a major mall, oftentimes, I would go shopping during my lunch hour. This mall consisted of many businesses, retail stores, restaurants, and pretty well everything working people might want at their fingertips.

On this particular day, I was having one of my "off" days. We all have these kinds of days now and then, but this one was particularly bad. As mentioned in some of my earlier chapters, I suffer from depression and I could sense that I was headed in that direction if I didn't take positive action. I decided I would go for a walk in the mall because I wasn't what one might consider to be "good company" in this rather foul mood of mine.

As I was walking along, I was wondering what I could do to cheer myself up and make for a better day. When I finally reached a section of the mall that had an outside door, I noticed a somewhat bedraggled man sifting through the sand in one of the big ashtrays near the entrance to the mall. There was no smoking allowed in this huge underground facility so anyone that came through the door had to "butt out".

It was obvious to me that this poor man was searching for the longest butts in the ashtray so he could have a few good puffs. By the way he was dressed and by his actions, it was apparent to me that he could not afford to buy his own cigarettes. Just looking at him and what he was doing made me forget all about my woes and my bad day.

As I focused on him a light bulb went on in my head and I decided to do a good deed or a random act of kindness. Over twenty years ago, to my knowledge no one referred to these acts by that term, but it doesn't mean to say that they weren't happening just the same. I went up to this man and gently asked him to wait right where he was standing. He looked up at me and nodded his head in agreement.

I turned around and went into a nearby drugstore and bought a large package of cigarettes and some matches. This was a time when smoking wasn't as nearly frowned upon as it is today. After purchasing the cigarettes, I quickly walked back to where the man was standing and handed him my recent purchase, receipt and all. I didn't want anyone to think he had stolen the cigarettes should he be seen with them. I suggested that he enjoy his gift and perhaps share them with some of his friends. He was very pleased, but what he said after that, changed my mood for the whole day and many days afterward.

This was a Monday, and Mondays can be kind of blue at times, just as it was for me that particular day. When this less fortunate man thanked me for the cigarettes, he quickly added, "What are you doing next Monday?" I almost laughed out loud because I found his question so surprising and somewhat amusing. He completely caught me off guard. He was planning on meeting me there as often as possible, perhaps every Monday if I was willing. It was such a cute response. I couldn't help but smile at him as I told him that this was just a spontaneous, one time occurrence and I just wanted to make his day.

In essence the exact opposite happened, he made mine instead. By reaching out to someone with a greater need than my own and giving in such a small way, it made me realize that it truly is better to give than to receive. I was given so much that precious day because even after all these years, the memory of that incident still brings a smile to my face. By doing what I did, I discovered that *"no one is in charge of your happiness but you"*. *~ Regina Brett*

This little story reminded me of how fortunate I really was and how by going out of my way to make a less fortunate person have a good day, it actually ended up creating a better one for me. You really cannot give away a kindness in life.

The pleasure that this man had on his face was a hugely rewarding experience. He was very grateful and he thanked me for my kindness. However, it was me who had every reason to thank him for accepting my simple gift and getting me out of my funk. He was the one being kind and gracious. He did not get offended by my gesture. He made me smile and managed to elevate my mood by showing his gratefulness that blue Monday so many years ago.

"You may be dead broke and that's a reality, but in spirit you may be brimming over with optimism, joy, and energy. The reality of your life may result from many

outside factors, none of which you have control. Your attitudes, however, reflect the ways in which you evaluate what is happening." ~ *H. Stanley Judd*

Personal Reflections:

1. Do you ever have bad days?
2. If so, what do you usually do about it?
3. Have you created simple, little ways to help get yourself out of your "funks" before a deeper depression sets in?
4. Do you engage in random acts of kindness?

SAMPLE CHAPTER

A Woman's Voice ~ Volume 3

25 ~ Common Courtesy

"We find greatest joy, not in getting, but in expressing what we are...Men do not really live for honors or for pay; their gladness is not in the taking and holding, but in the doing, the striving, the building, the living. It is a higher joy to teach than to be taught. It is good to get justice, but better to do it; fun to have things but more to make them. The happy man is he who lives the life of love, not for the honors it may bring, but for life itself." ~ R. J. Baughan

"Courteous people learn courtesy from the discourteous." ~ Laura Fitzgerald

Does this quote from the book *Veil of Roses* by Laura Fitzgerald ring a bell with you or make any sense to you? It sure does to me. Common courtesy or common decency can be as uncommon as common sense. As you can see, I'm full of oxymorons as I take the opportunity to elaborate on this subject. What I am actually trying to say is this...when I witness people being rude or unkind to others, it really gets my goat. As soon as I observe such unacceptable behavior I always do a self-check. Subsequently, I almost bend over backwards to treat people with even more kindness than I normally do.

There is no way that I want to behave in such a discourteous or disrespectful manner. In essence, I immediately become even more courteous and behave the exact opposite of the negative behavior that I may have just observed. Therefore, the previous quote may actually be true in many instances. If people are discourteous in your presence, it may have a positive impact on your future behavior. My husband and I have a couple of cute expressions of our own. When we observe bad behavior my husband will often say…"if I ever act like that, please let me know" or "remind me 'not' to act in such a rude manner". What do you think? Do you also bend over backwards to 'not' act the same discourteous way that you may have witnessed?

I had a very rewarding conversation with one of my daughters a few years ago. At the end of the school year, my granddaughters were receiving their final report cards. This was an especially important end-of-the-year ceremony because they were in the process of moving to another city during the summer. My two oldest granddaughters were fifteen and twelve at the time and it created a period of adjustment for them. Although, my daughter realized that there would be a transition period, she had every reason to be optimistic. Both girls were doing well in school and had received academic awards in the past. At the finale of this particular year-end ceremonies, the younger daughter received this very unique award. It was titled the **WWJD** Award.

I reacted the very same way as my daughter did when she first heard the news that Becca was to receive this special award. I quickly asked, "What in the world does **WWJD** stand for"? This was her reply…"It stands for the "**W**hat **W**ould **J**esus **D**o Award" if He were in your shoes.

In essence, my granddaughter's classmates had nominated her for the award in recognition of the most Christ-like behavior observed by them in her interactions with her peer group. That sounds like a fine compliment to me. Wouldn't it be wonderful if our behavior emulated Christ's as well in our dealings with our own peer group?

On a similar note, sometime ago, my then two-year old granddaughter told me that I was her best friend. Wow…where does a two-year old hear such an expression? Well, she has three older siblings and I'm sure she heard it from one of them when they were talking either with or about their friends.

I was very touched when she made this comment, although, I'm not so sure she knew exactly what she was saying. Young children, usually go to great lengths and have much need for a best friend. It's all part of the growing up process. I'm pretty sure we have all been there.

As the years have gone by, I've come to realize that my younger girlish need for a best friend no longer exists. My best friend is my husband and all my female and male friends are just that, my friends. I love them, enjoy them, and I relish the relationships that we share.

Over the years as part of the maturation process, I have changed my focus. For many years now, my goal in life has been "to be" a best friend rather than "to have" a best friend based on some insecure need of mine. By doing so, I hope my aspiration of emulating my granddaughter in her **WWJD** behavior shines out as much as humanly possible. I have surrounded myself with a wonderful group of people, both female and male. I always try my best to be a true and loyal friend. I have every desire to take their feelings into consideration at every opportunity. Hopefully, one day my young granddaughter will realize that I am truly her best friend because I love her with all my heart. Isn't that what being a best friend is really all about? I sure hope so because my friends mean the world to me.

As I continue on this lighter note, I would like to add that I try to view life in the simplest of ways and to use my imagination as much as possible to explain my thoughts. This is the reason I use my personal experiences to make a variety of points. It is necessary for me to draw from this wealth of information in order to urge you to tap into your past and find the correlation between your life and what I am trying to say. This gives my readers a better chance of relating to my message and how it might apply in their own lives.

Here's another example of tapping into your imagination. Our lives can be as plain and simple as two slices of bread stuck together with butter or as exciting as the ingredients that we put into it. I much prefer what is between the slices of bread rather than the bread itself, although, I do enjoy good quality bread. In reality, I need both.

I want my sandwich so thick with meat and other fixings so that I can hardly wrap my mouth around it. This is the same way that I want to enjoy my life. I don't just want to be born and then eventually die. That's a given. In other words, I don't merely want to exist. I want a lot of in-between stuff to make a really good life for myself and for those around me.

I can settle for bread squeezed together with butter or margarine or I can have a huge "Dagwood" sandwich with all of my favorite things in the middle. It's up to me. As I said, I can settle for less or build my life in much the same way that I make my sandwiches, thick with messy and juicy flavors like pickles and peppers. I want to lead a full and rewarding life that is pleasing to my Maker. How about you? Would you be a possible candidate for the **WWJD Award?**

SAMPLE CHAPTER

Growing Up and Liking It

Chapter 3 ~ My *No* Means *No!*

Our oldest granddaughter is now fourteen years old. I can't tell you the pleasure that she brought us when she was born. I had no idea about the depth of love grandparents could feel for their grandchildren until I actually experienced it. We have had seven more grandchildren since that momentous day, and we still hope to exceed that number. Not unlike the love we have for our children, the love for our grandchildren is equally as great. Every grandchild has such a special place in our hearts whether the first, the middle, or the lastborn. It has been said that love multiplies; it doesn't divide. I can vouch for that statement because it certainly has in the love we have known for our children and our grandchildren. I also know that love multiplies in all instances where it is present, not only with our families, but in other relationships as well. True love does not cause resentment, bitterness, or family friction. True love grows and embraces others in such a way that no one feels short-changed or robbed of their fair share of it.

When our oldest granddaughter was two years old, she was experiencing the terrible twos. It is the stage of life when a young child hears a lot of the word *no*. I have a grandson who is now two years old, and he is also hearing the word *no* often. I also notice that he is using it more than his fair share. At times, it can be seen as a battle of the wills, as he refuses to do what is asked of him. I smile to myself because he is so strong-willed and defiant, but on the outside I remind him that my *no* means *no*. His parents are reminding him on a daily basis, so I must follow suit when he spends time with us to make sure that we are on the same page as far as what is acceptable or unacceptable behavior. We all know that these two-year-olds understand the meaning of the word *no*. We also know that a lot of the times they just want to defy the authority behind the word. When our first grandchild was two years old, our daughter utilized the expression, "My 'no' means 'no'" quite often.

One time in particular the reverse happened. My husband and I were visiting them, and we were laughing and tickling our then two-year-old granddaughter. The more she seemed to enjoy it, the more we wanted to just squeeze her and tickle her some more. I guess it got into the point where she had had enough because she said *no* to us so that we would stop. We thought that we were still playing the "tickle me" game, so we proceeded to tickle her one more time. She turned around and looked at us and said in no uncertain terms, "My 'no' means 'no.'" Even at the young age of two we knew she meant it. We respected her wishes, and we stopped tickling her. If she not only understood those words at such a young age but could effectively use them and get the results she wanted, why does the proper use of this word elude some adults? It has been my experience that few people realize the appropriateness and, at times, very valuable need to actually use the word *no*. Saying *yes* to everything all of the time is no more appropriate than saying *no* all of the time, regardless of your age. It's perfectly okay to say *no*, at least some of the time, if you have a good reason for doing so. If you are uncomfortable with a person/situation or what is being done to you or asked of you, just say *no*! If you are not taken seriously the first time, just like our young granddaughter, look the person straight in the eye and say, "My 'no' means 'no.'" We heard her loud and clear.

    Did you know that discipline has been said to be one of the greatest forms of love? When someone is saying *no* to us, it may actually be for our own good or for theirs. It seems to me that we have confused the meaning of a lot of words in the English language. I don't know how many times the word *no* is used incorrectly. At times it is used to actually mean the word *maybe*. Similarly, others may use the word *yes* but they actually mean *no* or vice versa. It is necessary to have a good look at these three simple words of *yes, no,* and *maybe,* and make every effort to use them appropriately. When we really mean what we say, there will be little or no room for confusion. The misuse of these three simple little words can end up getting most of us into a lot of hot water. "Mean what you say" and "Say what you mean" are handy mottos to use in everyday living. By walking to the beat of this drum, we benefit by having more open and honest relationships. This results in better communication with others. There is a big up side to this type of communication because it is better for all the people involved to know what the boundaries are in a mutually respectful relationship.

We eventually end up with a lot of positive things like self-respect, mutual respect, personal responsibility, and also accountability when it comes to our own actions. "Success on any major scale requires you to accept responsibility…in the final analysis, the one quality that all successful people have…is the ability to take on responsibility."[i] I have a beautiful message that I would like to share with you. It was written by Whitney Griswold and adds to what I have to say in an incredible way. "Self respect cannot be hunted. It is never for sale. It cannot be purchased. It cannot be fabricated out of public relations. It comes when we are alone, in quiet moments, in quiet places, when we suddenly realize that, knowing the good, we have done it; knowing the beautiful, we have served it; knowing the truth we have spoken it."[ii] Don't you just love the words in this message? I sure do. When we have self-respect, it gives us the desire, the confidence, and the ability to effectively use the word *no*. It is our God-given right to be able to say *no* even if there are negative consequences.

When you develop self-respect, the inner positive effects for standing up for yourself or what you believe in more than make up for any negative fall out which may result from saying *no*. I know that it sounds simple to use this little two-letter word, but it is actually quite difficult. First of all, we have to practice our use of it. When we use the word *no*, it must always mean *no*. There can be no exceptions. If at a later date, we change our minds from a *no* to a *yes*, we must take the time to explain why we have changed our response. If we don't, we lose some of our credibility. For example, we should use the word *maybe* if we are unsure, and we should utilize the words *yes or no* if we are sure. When we properly use these three simple little words in the English language, those around us know where they stand. If the people around us also used these three little words the same way, we would all know where we stand with each other. John D. Rockefeller, Jr. said, "I will pay more for the ability to deal with people that any other ability under the sun."[iii] His words are a pretty strong indication of how difficult getting along with people actually can be. There would be a lot less frustration in our lives if we all followed this simple advice. "Hold yourself responsible for a higher standard than anybody else expects of you. Never excuse yourself."[iv] It is up to each and every one of us to make every effort to develop responsible behavior when dealing with those around us. Our words are so important, but two of the smallest yet most important ones are *yes* and *no*. When we give our word it is necessary to keep it in order to have both self-respect and the respect of others.

Step 3 Make sure that you "mean what you say" and "say what you mean". If your "*no* means *no*" stand by it! People will eventually take you at your word and your self-esteem and self-respect will increase, thereby allowing you to command more respect from others. Once again, here are a few more questions that you can ask yourself to better benefit from my simple suggestion of recognizing the difference between "mean what you say" and "say what you mean". Often times, the difference is ever so subtle, therefore, it is necessary to be really tuned in to your inner self. When we are more honest with ourselves, we end up with more honest relationships with others. Do you remember a time when you said *no* but meant *yes*. Or when you committed to an engagement that you knew you weren't going to make? How did that make you feel? Try planning your days so that you can be sure to allow enough time for your family, friends, and yourself! This will help enhance your ability to be true to your word and true to yourself.

---

[i] "Michael Korda quotes," Thinkexist.com,
http://thinkexist.com/quotes/michael_korda/.
[ii] ".Whitney. Griswold quotes," Eugene C. Gerhart, Quote It Completely (Buffalo, New York: Wm.S.Hein Publishing, 1998), P.960.
[iii] "John D. Rockefeller quotes," the painter's key,
http://quote.robertgenn.com/getquotes.php?catid=1.
[iv] "Henry Ward Beecher quotes," BrainyQuote,
http://www.brainyquote.com/quotes/authors/h/henry_ward_beesher.html.

TO CONTACT AUTHOR:

WEBSITE

http://www.doloresayotte.com

BLOG SITE

http://www.doloresayotte.wordpress.com

FACEBOOK AUTHOR'S PAGE

http://www.facebook.com/Author.Dolores.Ayotte

www.ingramcontent.com/pod-product-compliance
Lightning Source LLC
Chambersburg PA
CBHW071302040426
42444CB00009B/1833